Who Ha

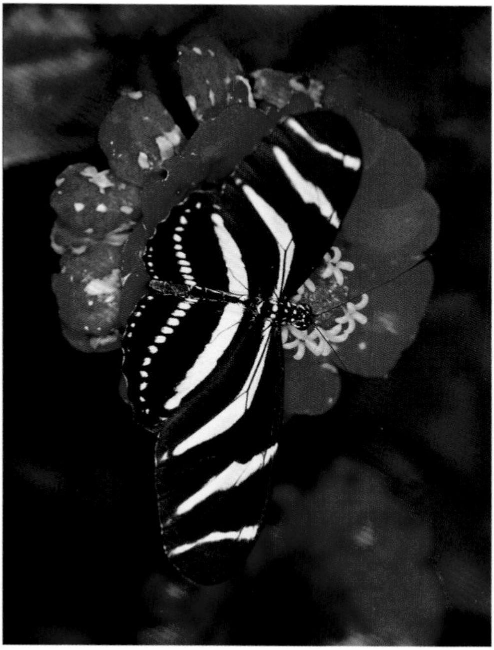

written by Pam Holden

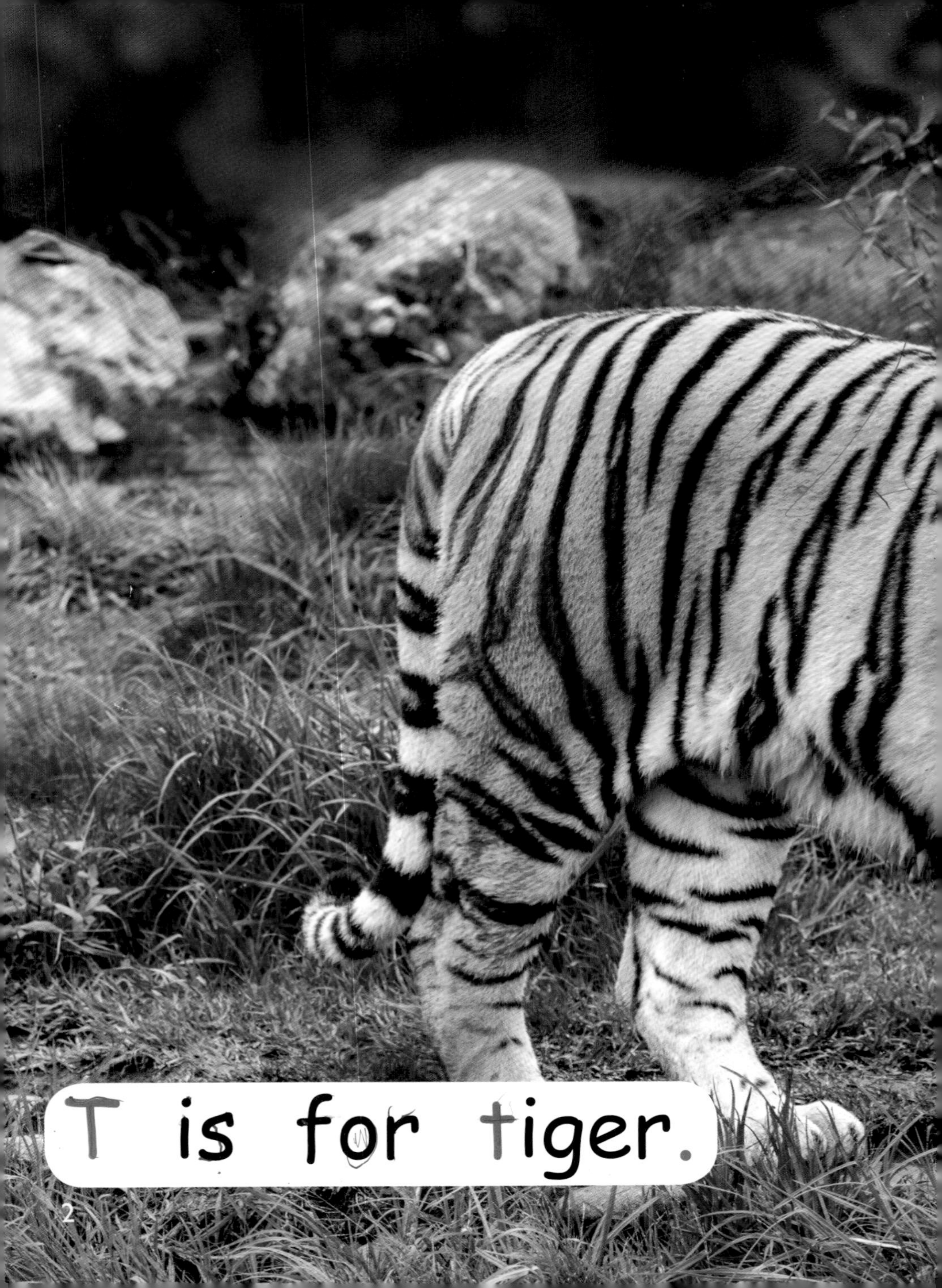

T is for tiger.

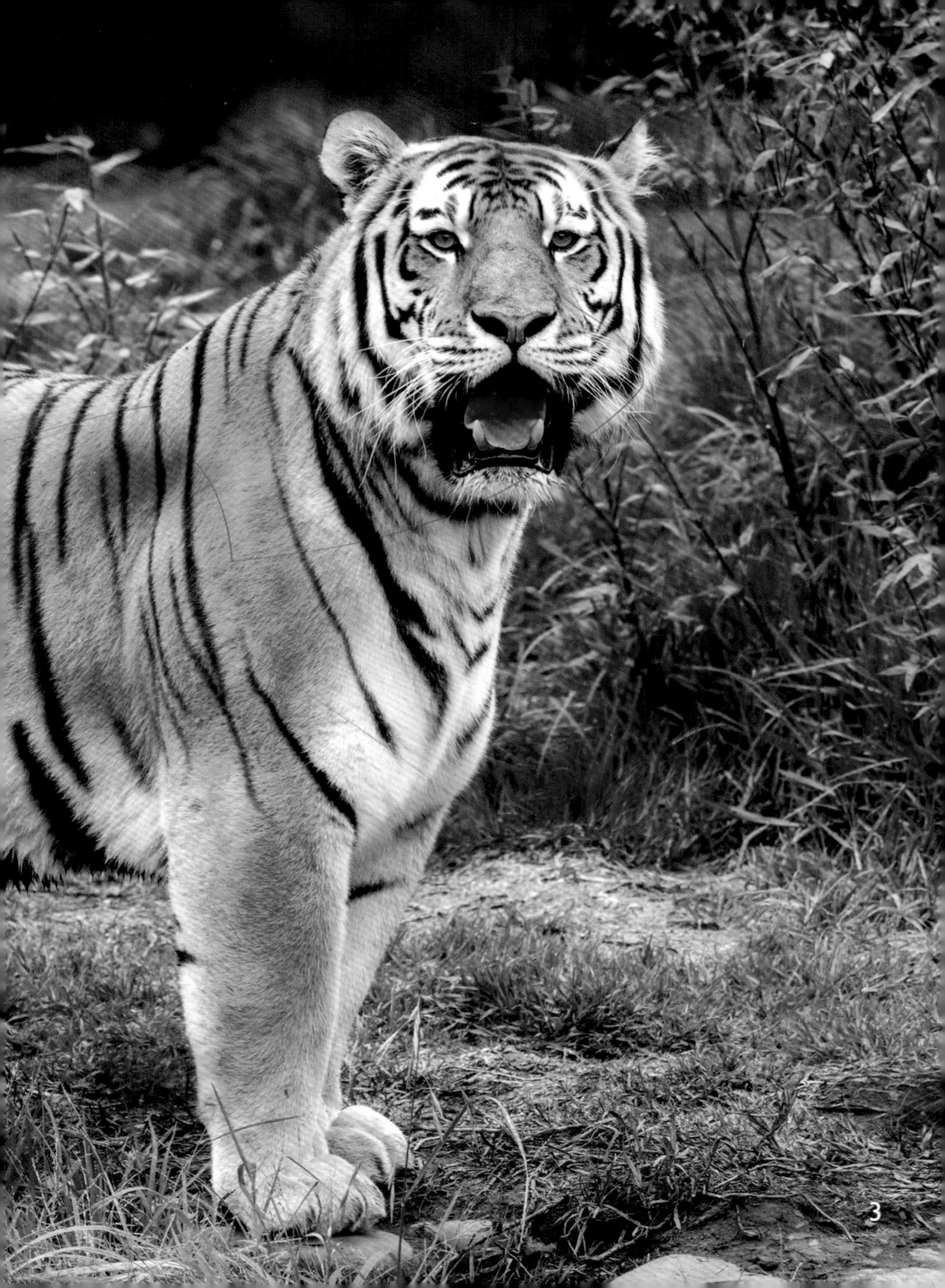

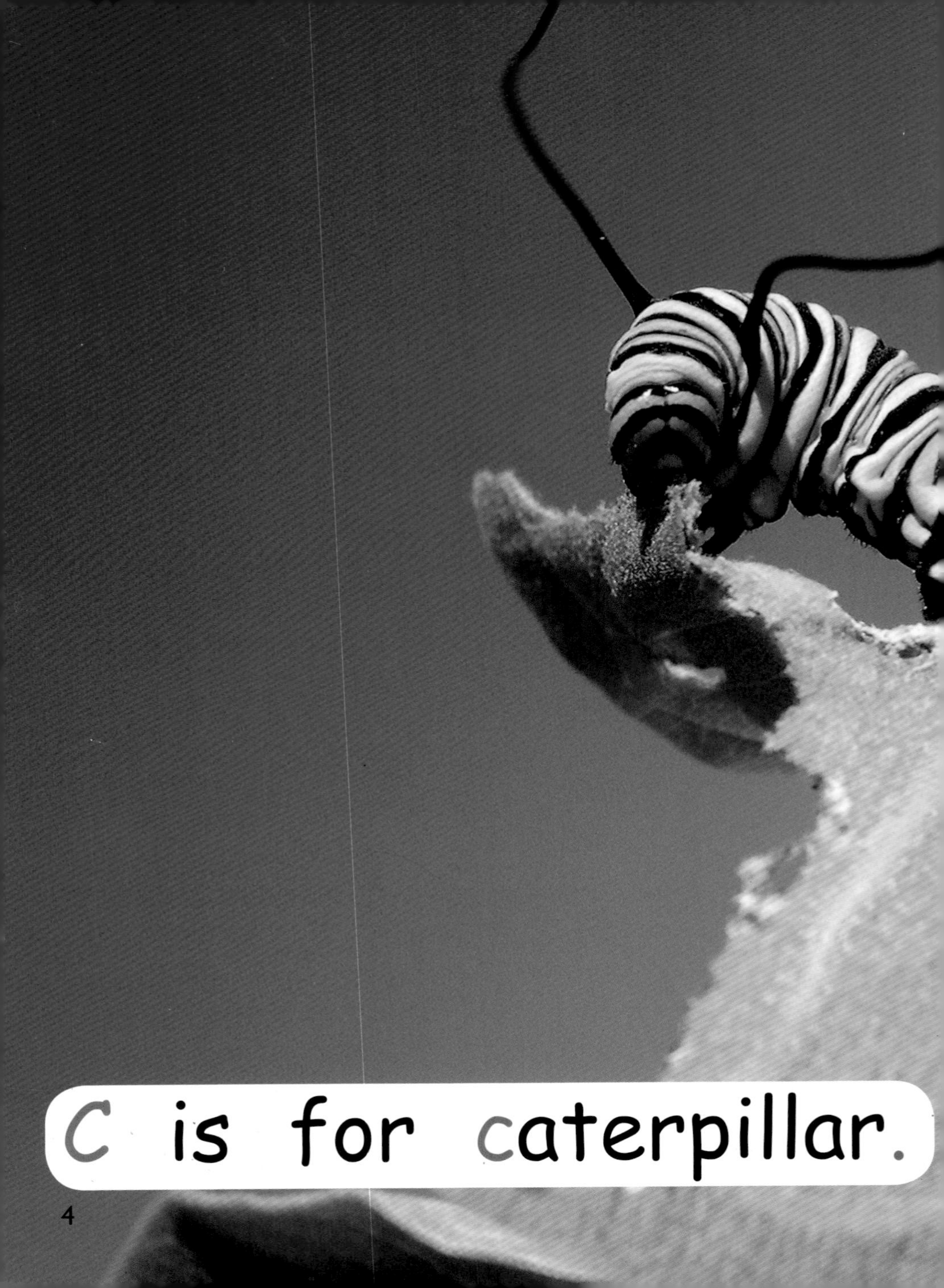

C is for caterpillar.

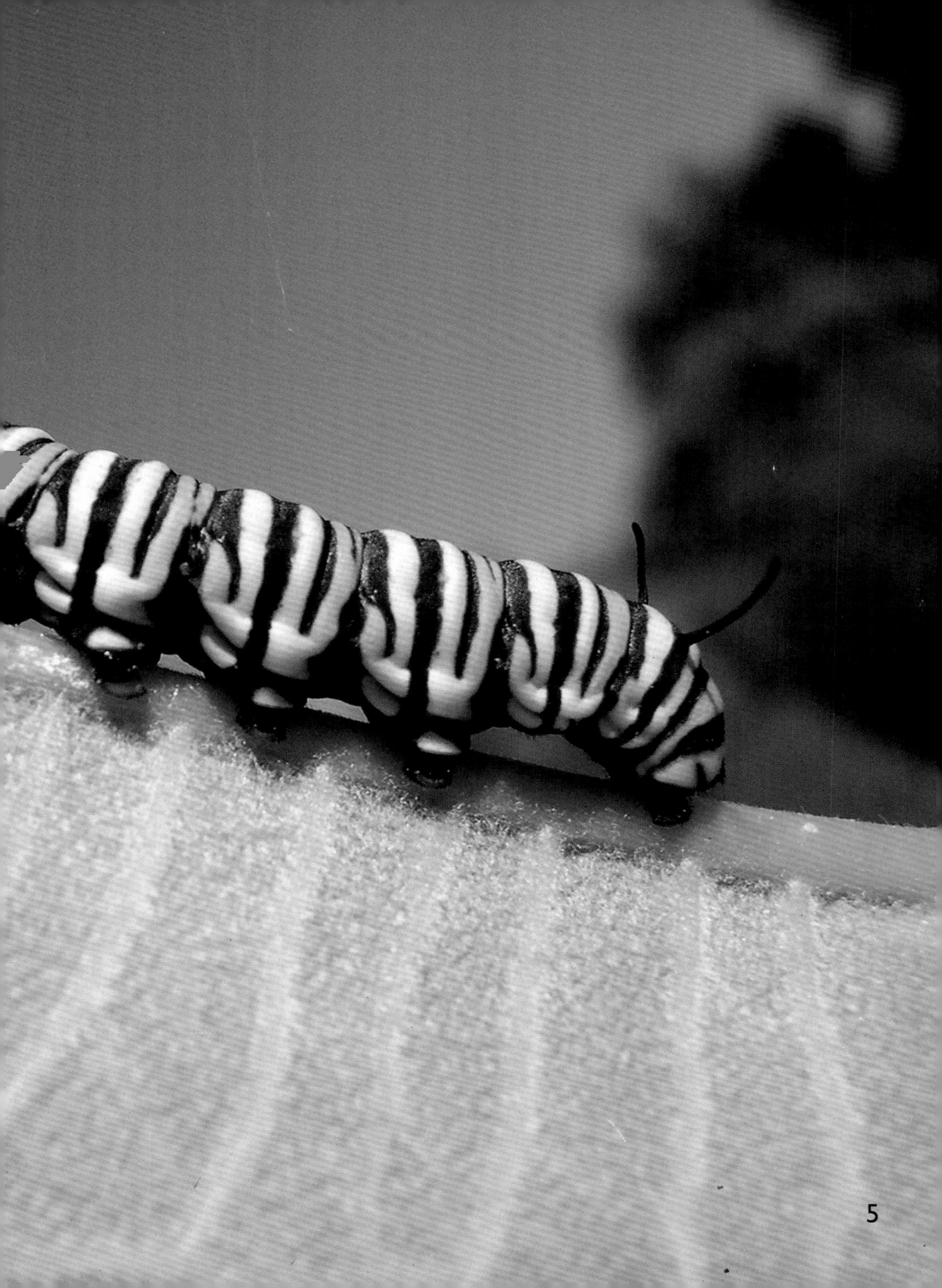

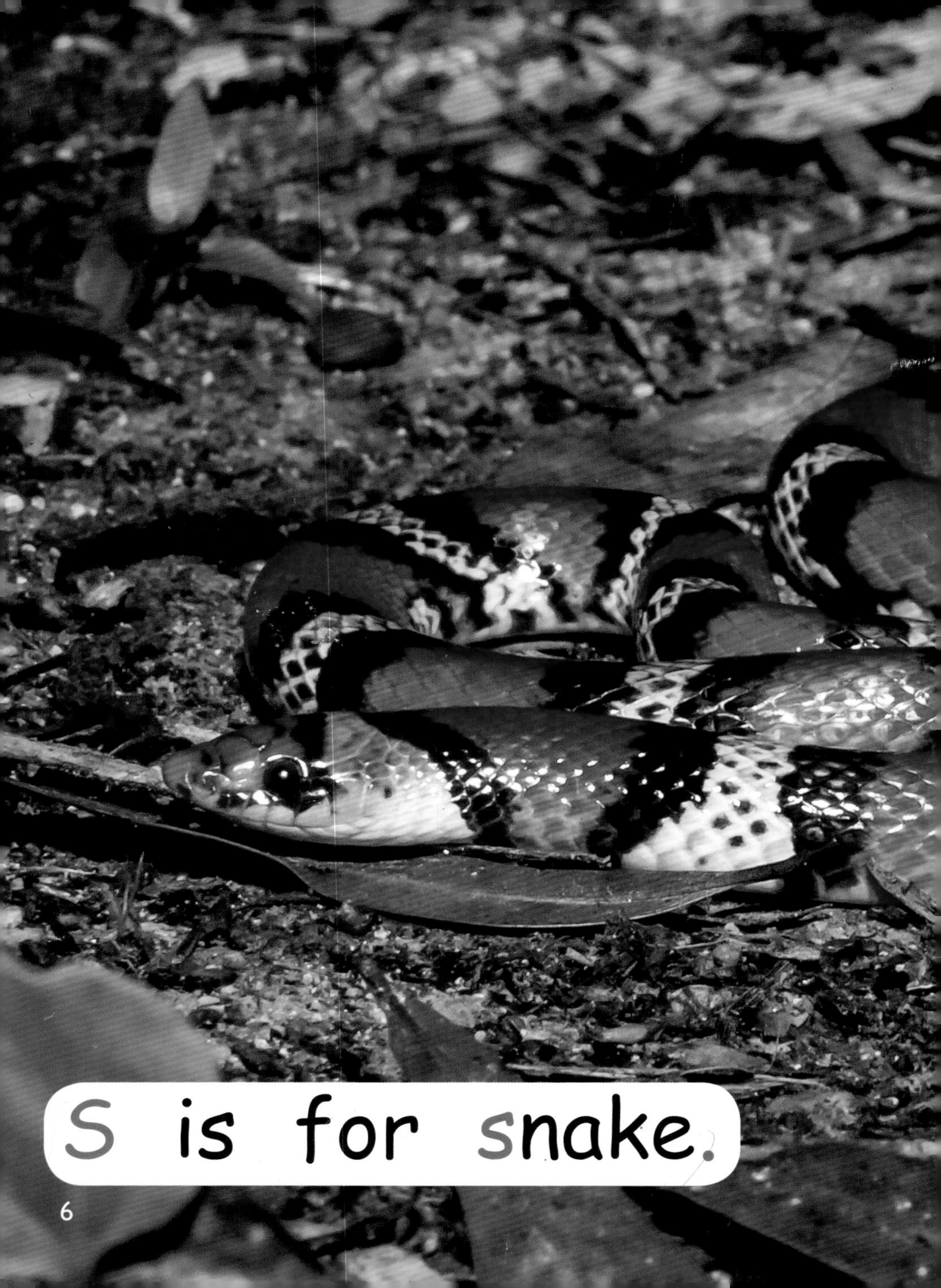

S is for snake.

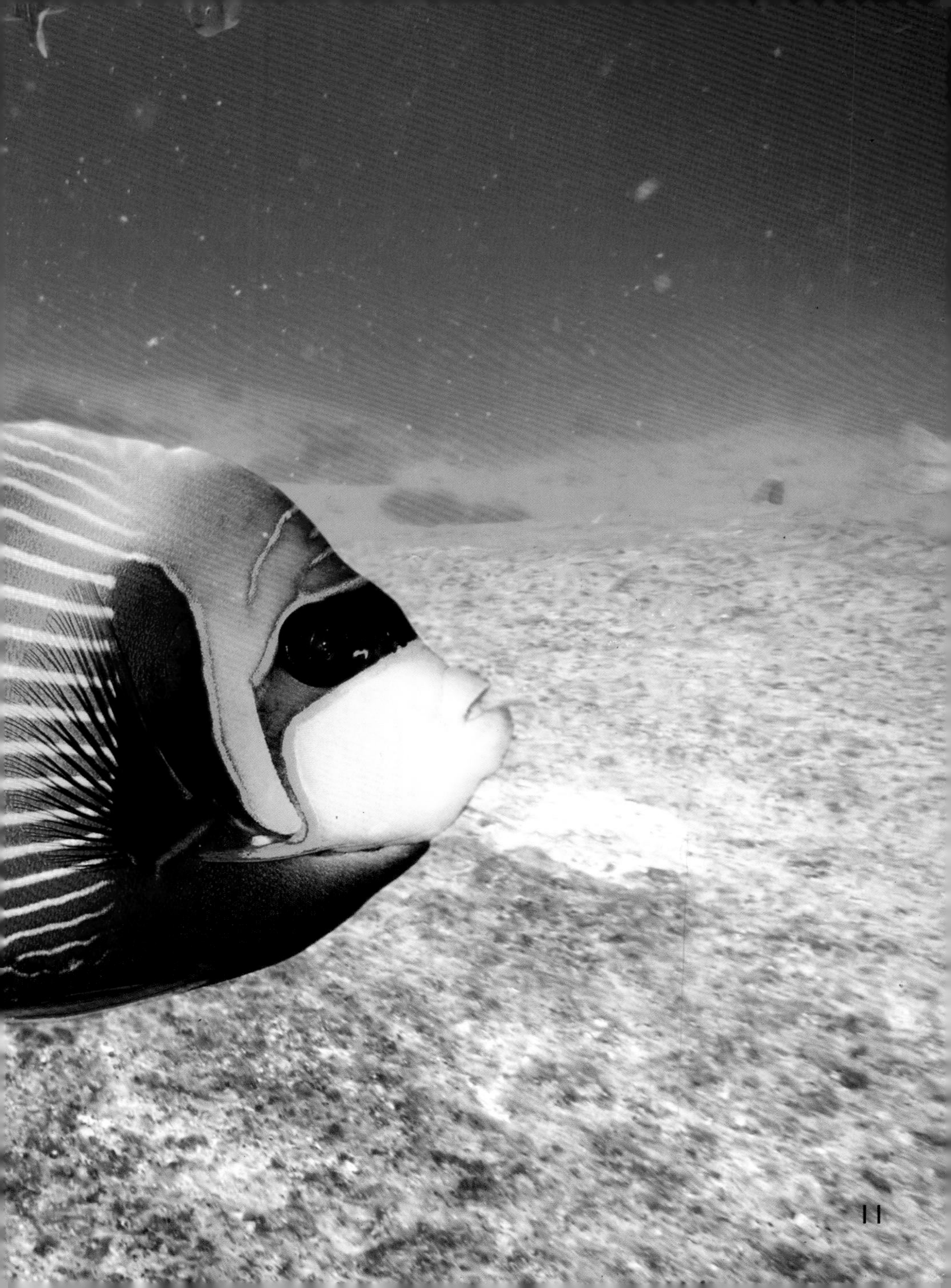

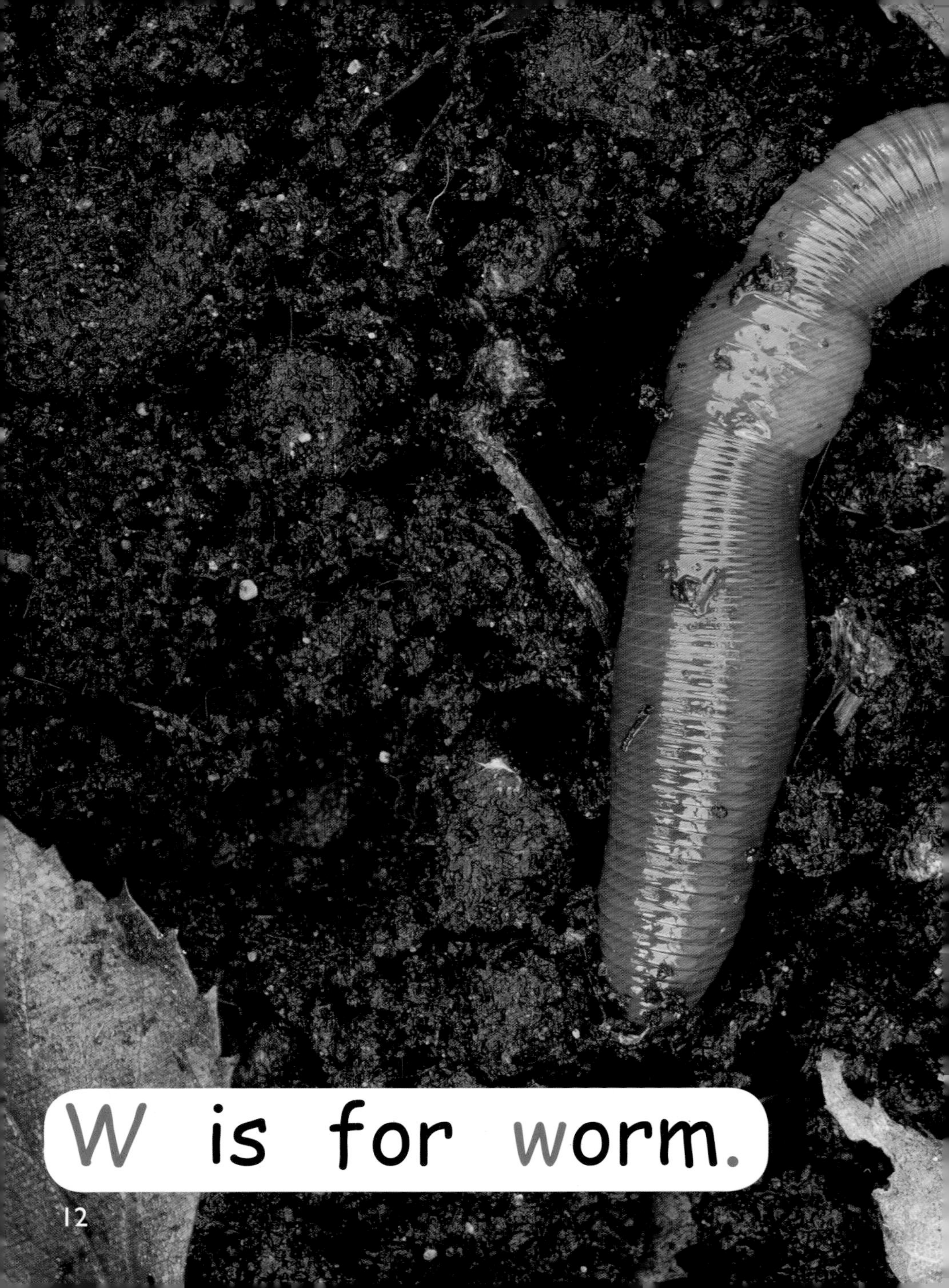

W is for worm.

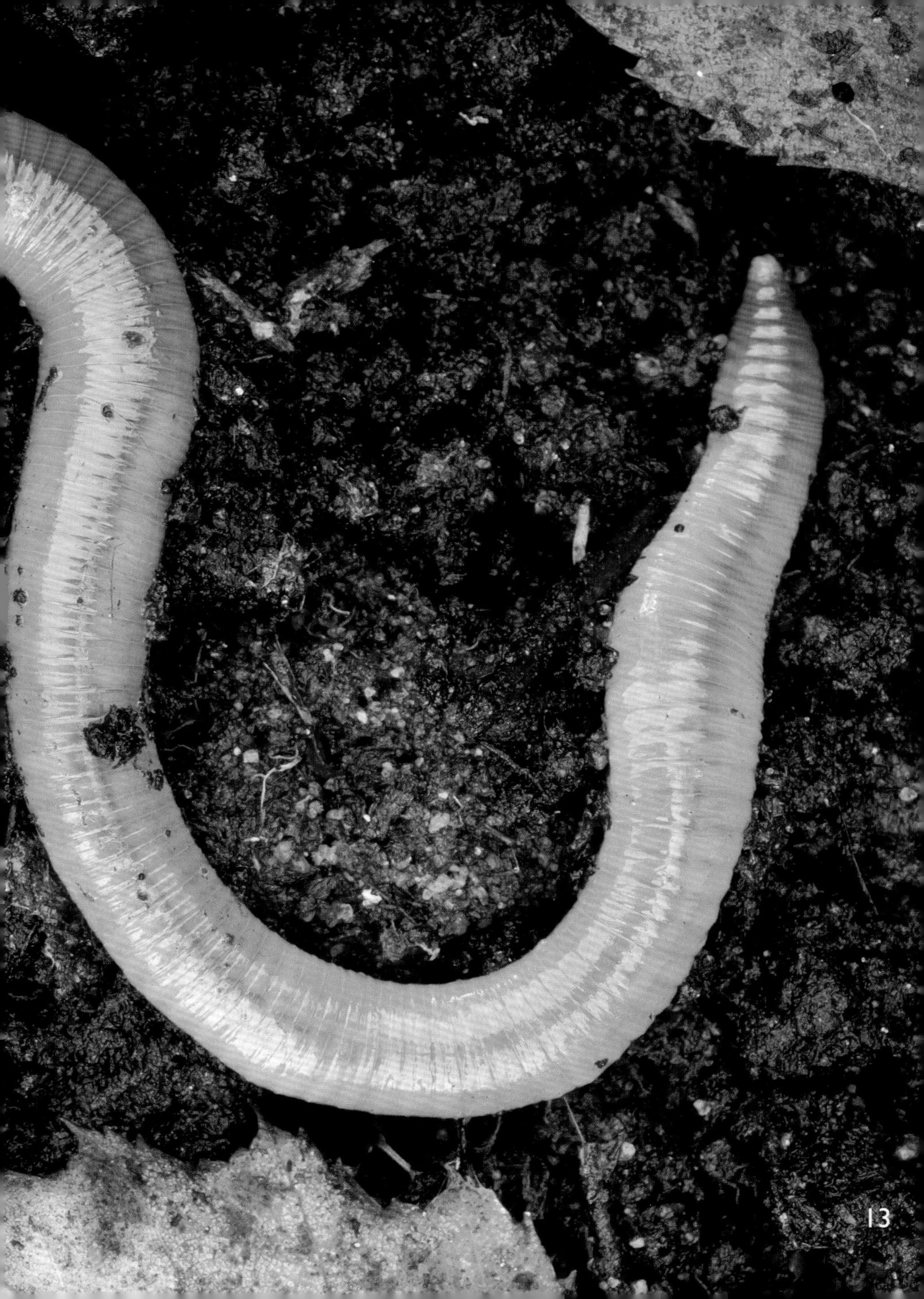

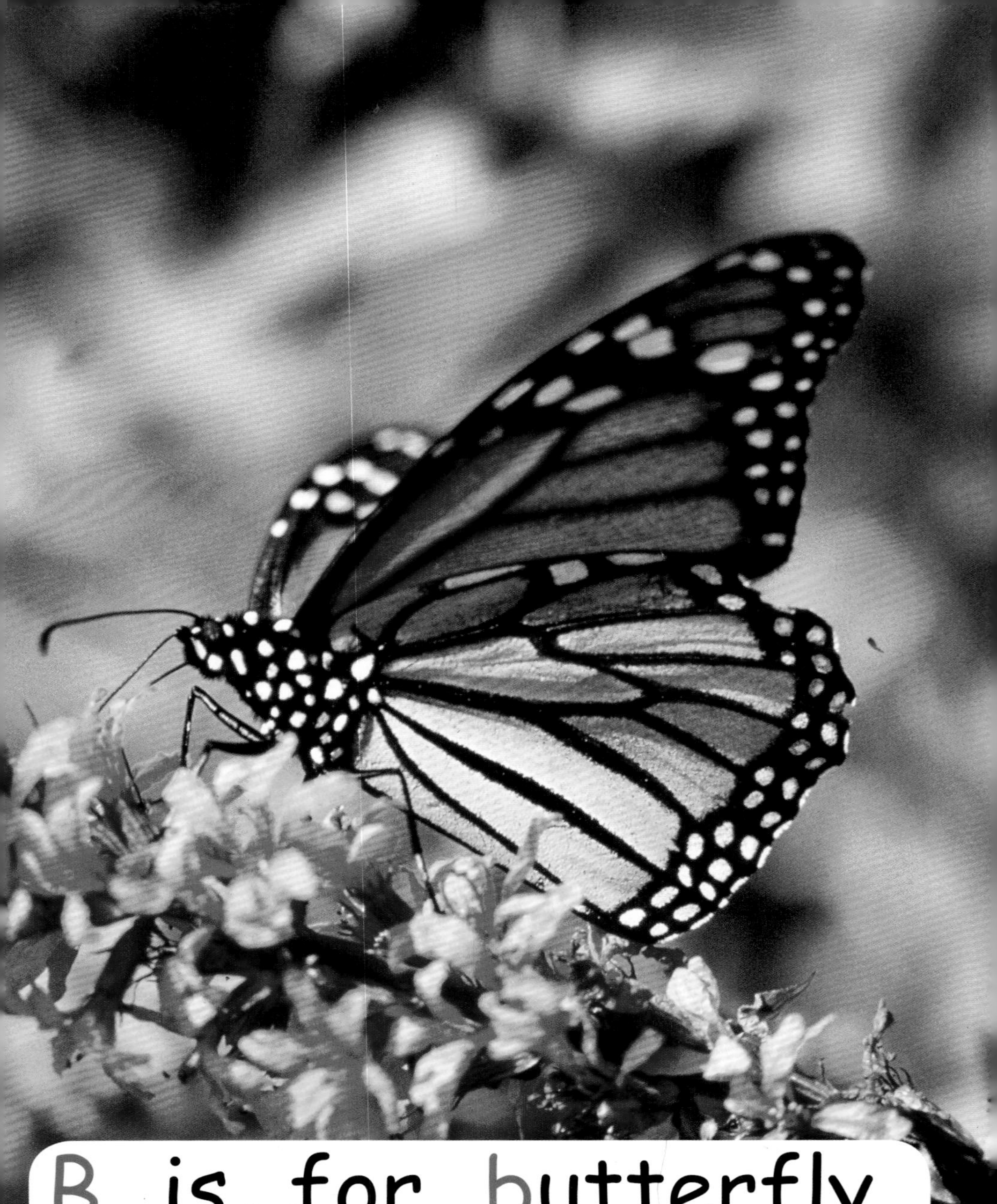

B is for butterfly

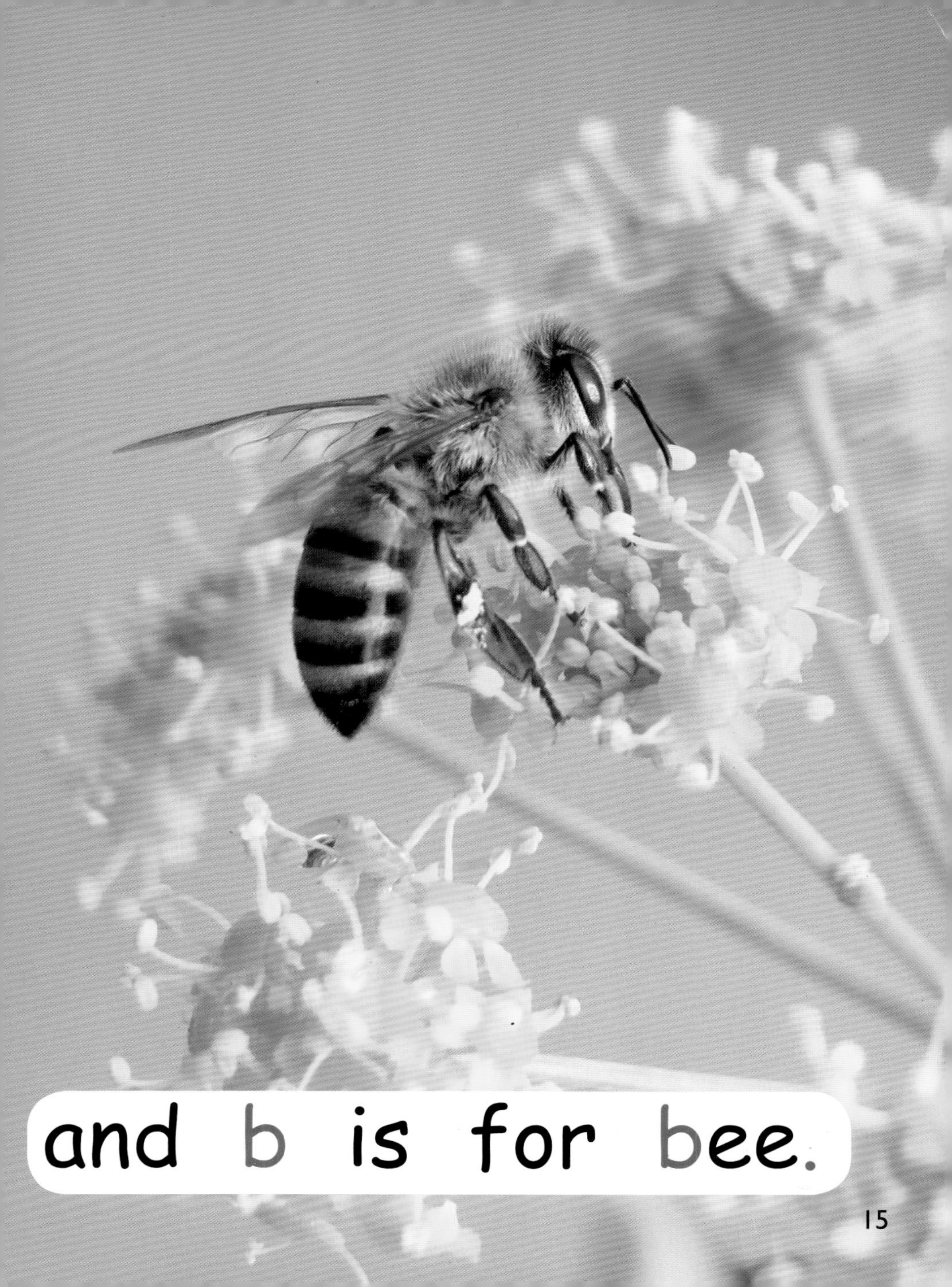

and b is for bee.

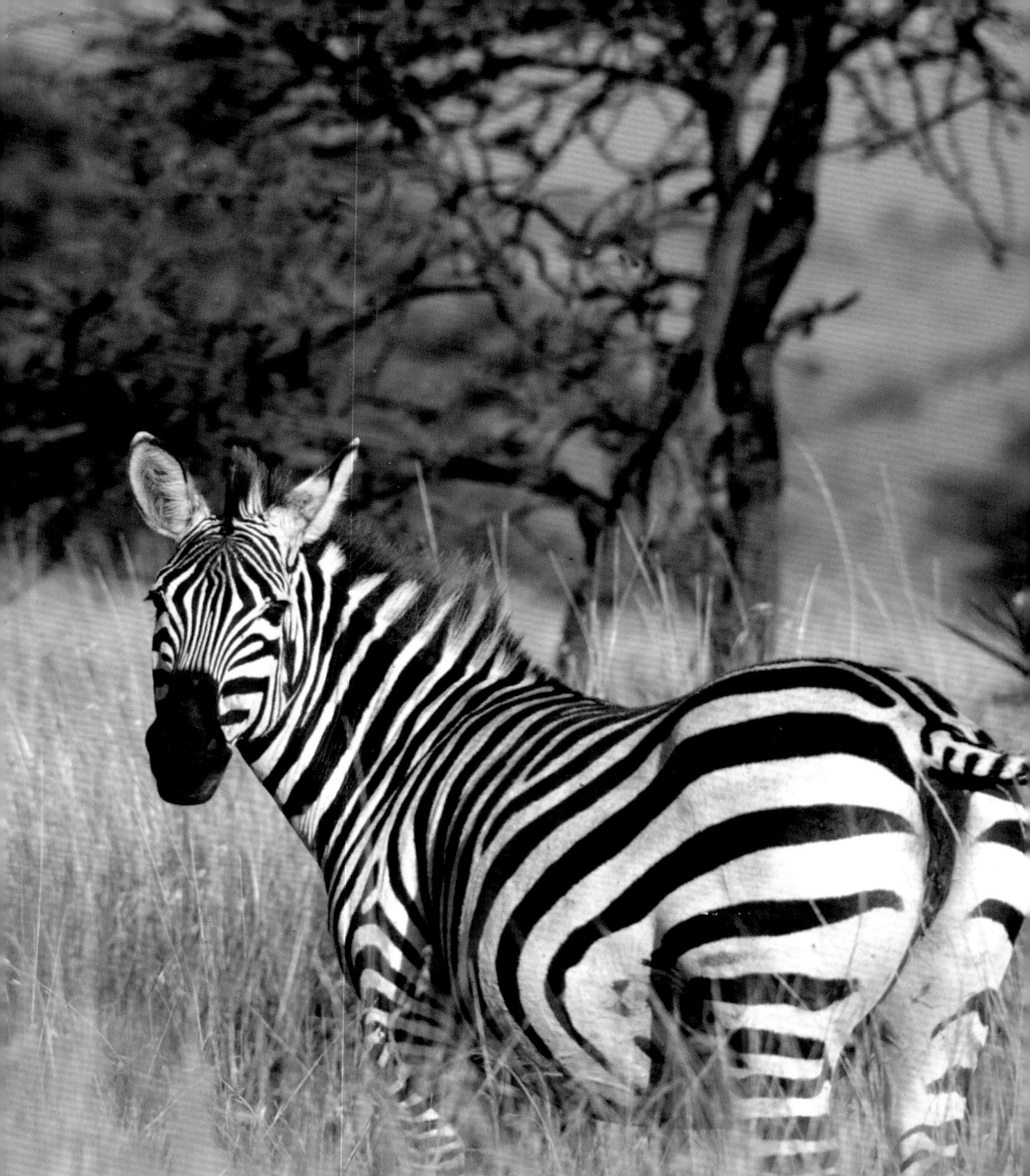

Z is for zebra.